IF I WERE A...

BIRD

WRITTEN BY
CHARIS MATHER

WINDMILL BOOKS

Published in 2025 by Windmill Books,
an Imprint of Rosen Publishing
2544 Clinton St.
Buffalo, NY 14224

Written by:
Charis Mather

Edited by:
E.C. Andrews

Designed by:
Ker Ker Lee

Cataloging-in-Publication Data
Names: Mather, Charis, 1999-.
Title: Bird / Charis Mather.
Description: Buffalo, NY : Windmill Books, 2025. | Series: If I were a… | Includes glossary and index.
Identifiers: ISBN 9781538398012 (pbk.) | ISBN 9781538398029 (library bound) | ISBN 9781538398036 (ebook)
Subjects: LCSH: Birds--Juvenile literature.
Classification: LCC QL676.2 M376 2025 | DDC 598--dc23

Printed in the United States of America

CPSIA Compliance Information: Batch #CW25WM
For Further Information contact Rosen Publishing at 1-800-237-9932

Find us on

Photo Credits – Images are courtesy of Shutterstock.com. With thanks to Getty Images, Thinkstock Photo and iStockphoto.

Characters – yusufdemirci. Recurring images – Sachiko Nakai. Cover – Ondrej Prosicky, Phillip Rubino, Alan Tunnicliffe, PaniYani. 2–3 – Ondrej Prosicky. 4–5 – SARATSTOCK. 6–7 – FotoRequest, Svoboda Pavel. 8–9 – Smit, Stacey Ann Alberts, tahirsphotography. 10–11 – laura.h, Ludmila Yilmaz, Nicholas Richards. 12–13 – Jason Benz Bennee, Ken Griffith, nataniki. 14–15 – Harry Collins Photography, ridjam. 16–17 – Albert Beukhof, Andrew M. Allport, arjmA, Elena Istomina. 18–19 – Richard Seeley, ukrit.wa. 20–21 – David Herraez Calzada, George Vollmy.

CONTENTS

Words that look like this can be found in the glossary on page 24.

BRILLIANT BIRDS

It must be brilliant to be a bird.

A BIRD IS A CREATURE THAT HAS WINGS AND A BEAK.

Some birds are plain, and some are brightly colored. Some birds spend most of their time in the air, while others prefer being on land or in the water.

If you were a bird, what would you be? Would you be something with a beautiful singing voice? Or would you rather focus on flying? Whatever your interests, there are thousands of birds to choose from.

OWL

Owls have supersharp senses that help them hunt. They have the best nighttime eyesight of any bird. Even when prey is hidden, owls can find out where it is using their excellent hearing.

The round shape of some owls' faces helps them hear better.

Thanks to their specially shaped wings, some owls are nearly silent when they fly. This means that their prey cannot hear their wings flapping as they swoop down to catch them.

WEAVER

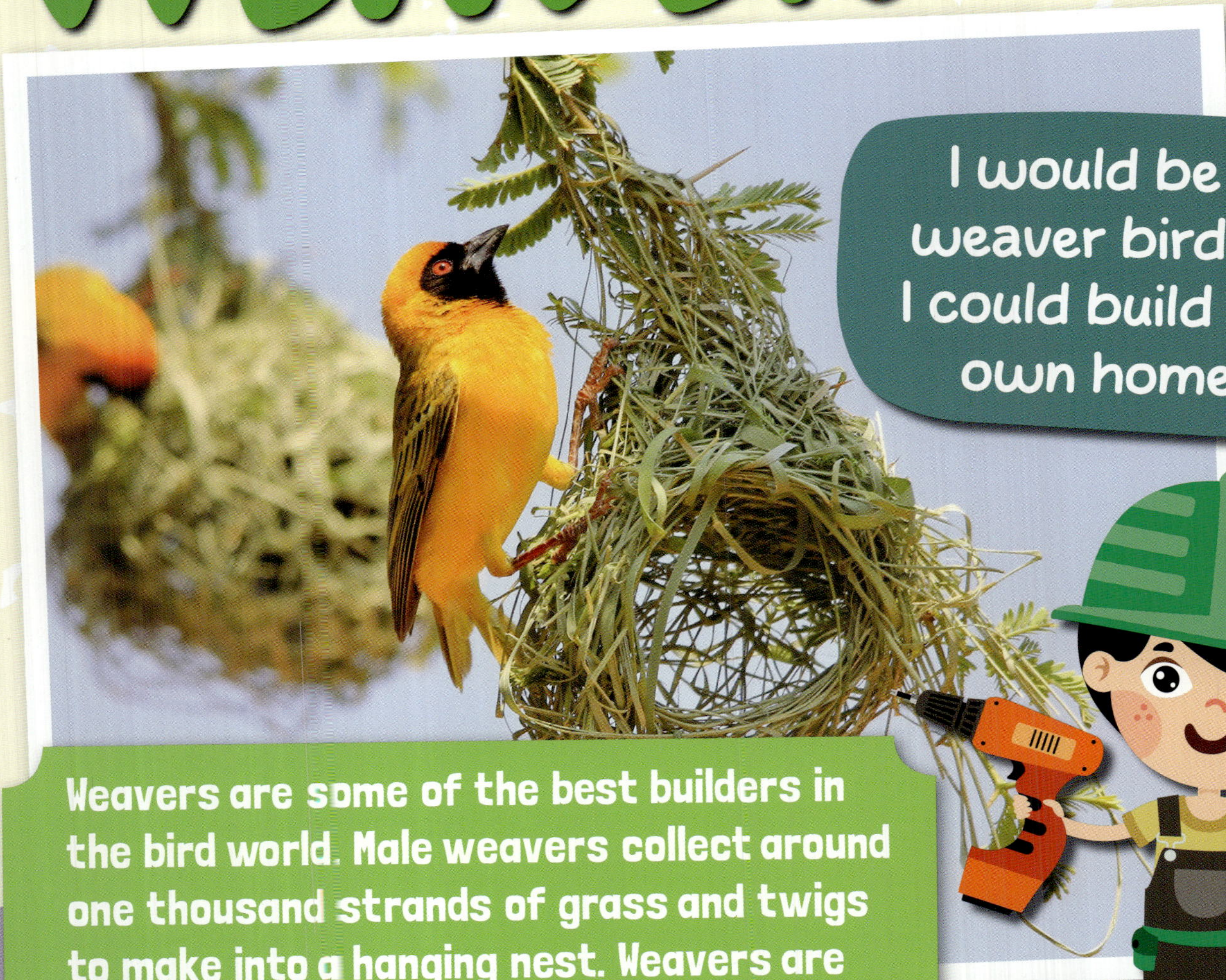

Weavers are some of the best builders in the bird world. Male weavers collect around one thousand strands of grass and twigs to make into a hanging nest. Weavers are the only birds that can tie knots.

Some weavers live in big groups called colonies. Together, they can form giant shared nests that can be home to hundreds of birds. These giant nests help protect weavers from predators and bad weather.

SOME GIANT NESTS CAN BE OVER A HUNDRED YEARS OLD.

FLAMINGO

The bright pink color of flamingos comes from their food. Baby flamingos have white-gray feathers when they are born. The more red, orange, and yellow foods they eat, the pinker they become.

To get their food, flamingos stand in the water and dip their heads in upside down. They suck in a mouthful of muddy water, then pump out anything that is not food.

Flamingos can often be found in very large colonies.

LYREBIRD

Lyrebirds are amazing at mimicking. This means that they can make noises that sound exactly like something else. Lyrebirds usually mimic natural sounds, but they can also mimic unnatural sounds, such as instruments or cars.

Although lyrebirds do have wings, they mostly stay on the ground. This is where they look for food. They usually go up into the trees to rest for the night.

Lyrebirds have long, striped tail feathers.

PEREGRINE FALCON

Peregrine falcons can speed through the air at around 200 miles (320 km) per hour. That is nearly three times as fast as a sprinting cheetah! Peregrine falcons are the fastest animals in the world.

Peregrine falcons are fastest when they are diving to catch prey. When they are high up in the air, falcons tuck their wings in so that they do not slow them down.

STARLING

From far away, starlings may look black, but they are actually much more colorful. In certain light, starlings have a green and purple shine to them. Starlings also have lots of small white spots.

When starlings fly in large groups, they look like dark clouds. These clouds of starlings are known as murmurations. As the starlings fly, the murmuration swirls into many different shapes.

HUMMINGBIRD

Some of the smallest birds in the world are hummingbirds. These little birds are not just amazing because of their small size. They also have some unique flying abilities.

Hummingbirds flap their wings so quickly that they hum.

Hummingbirds can fly in ways that no other birds can. They can fly sideways, backwards, and even upside down for a little while! They can hover in one spot while they feed.

PENGUIN

Not all birds can fly. Penguin wings are too short to lift these heavy birds into the air. Penguins spend a lot of time in water, so their wings are more useful as flippers.

Penguin colonies in cold places work together to survive. When the weather gets really cold, penguins huddle together to share each other's warmth. They swap places when the penguins on the outside get too cold.

WHAT WOULD YOU BE?

If I were a bird, I would be...

...as good at seeing in the dark as an owl.

...as pink as a flamingo.

...as brilliant at building as a weaver.

...as good at mimicking as a lyrebird.

...as good at group flying as a starling.

...as fantastic at flying as a hummingbird.

...as fast as a peregrine falcon.

...as good at swimming as a penguin.

What would you be?

GLOSSARY

hover to float in the air

natural found in nature and not made by people

predators animals that hunt other animals for food

prey animals that are hunted by other animals for food

senses things such as sight, smell, taste, and touch that help people or animals experience the world

survive to stay alive

unique unlike anything else

INDEX